A DISTANCE APART

A Distance Apart, Bill Mayer, poems copyright © 2019, Bill Mayer
All rights reserved, Marrowstone Press 2019

ISBN: 978-0-578-60270-7

cover photograph, 'The Tree,' by Galen Garwood, 2008

A DISTANCE APART

BILL MAYER
poems

MARROWSTONE PRESS

A DISTANCE APART

One: The Sequence 1
Two: *Pain was my blessing. I walked, or rather stumbled* 2
Three: *The photograph showed a small blond boy standing outside* 3
Four: Entr'acte 4
Five: Difficult 5
Six: *Faith in healing, the ability of the body* 6
Seven: *Look around less. Imagine more* 7
Eight: *I think I must have been a bird. Then maybe* 8
Nine: *When I woke up* 9
Ten: After Reading Faulkner's THE BEAR 10
Eleven: *Dreaming is useful, handy when needed* 11
Twelve: *Questions, always questions. I have them all the time* 12
Thirteen: The Practice 13
Fourteen: *How can a puma be a rock? Or history be tomorrow?* 15
Fifteen: *Poetry can't do it, unfortunately* 16
Sixteen: *Talking about last things* 17
Seventeen: Primary Colors 20
Eighteen: *Now I'm traveling on the caboose* 21
Nineteen: Happiness 22
Twenty: Another Guide 23
Twenty-one: *You have to ask; purity, if that is what you want* 24
Twenty-two: *If there is no dissonance, only a greater definition* 25
Twenty-three: The Explorer 26
Twenty-four: *There is a sliding panel at the corner of my left eye* 27
Twenty-five: The Magnificent Tree 28
Twenty-six: *Guests come. I can't tell if they are saving my life* 29

One

The Sequence

In the latter part of life, I found myself lost, baffled,
and having no idea what to do. All that I thought I knew
seemed false; all that I had relied upon mistaken.
I stood as at the entrance of a forest without guides, maps or GPS.
Suddenly I had become careful, confused, and full of doubt.
My doctor then told me the most important quality
I needed for healing was confidence.
Who or what could help me now? Who could lead me
through my own dark wood? It is true the trees had become sparser
with age, and dryer. I had been walking down a steep canyon
that had become trailless, on the east slope.
That put me in the rain shadow; lodgepole became Jeffrey,
Jeffrey became piñon, and then, beyond that,
a broad valley of mesquite and ironwood,
which strangely became darker, not clearer, as expected,
though the sun was high and the air sweet.
Everything was as it should be, but nothing was familiar;
all was strange, as though I'd been transported to the steppes.
Look, I've tried to live my life according to what mattered,
against the advice of almost everyone. I had followed
what I knew to be true; I'd had masters, been almost incredibly fortunate.
When Jack had asked, first thing, how important poetry was to us,
I wrote down some nonsense about how much it mattered
but that I was going to have to live in the real world
and get a job, and maybe a career. He made me suffer for that,
and I've never forgotten it. I took the hard lessons
with the easy and never regretted a thing. So now, what was I doing
lost in a great expanse of cacti and the distant empty hills?

Two

Pain was my blessing. I walked, or rather stumbled
down the canyon. The birds stopped, but silence
eluded me. Instead a chaotic chattering, as though
I were in a crowded restaurant, the glasses clinking
and the drinks flowing. Not one word could I hear,
but all words were spoken, and in all languages.
Smell of sweat and frustrated people, hungry
for what they did not have. I closed my eyes
and walked slowly ahead, avoiding somehow the chollas,
avoiding another person. My feet hurt.
As though my body was deciding just to quit,
lay down and give up, my time over.
An artist, a man, a failure said e. e. cummings,
and at least the last part rang true.

Three

The photograph showed a small blond boy standing outside,
the distant orange grove valley behind, down the hill.
It is strange, thinking how I thought myself to be then,
hearing that boy inside as though it were a week ago,
having no perspective or distance, but being him now,
smiling, a gap where a tooth had fallen out and the new one
was beginning to replace it. I know what he thought. It is
what I still think, age of no consequence, time irrelevant.
A boy living in books and his imagination, the next door lot
a jungle to explore, a treehouse until the neighbors complained,
then an underground fort, and poison oak to catch.
Whatever was magic then remains so today, fresh and vital.
Having no idea of the great, yawning gap I was about to enter,
always entering, never leaving, always in the center of my life.

Four

Entr'acte

I came slowly out of meditation not at all certain
whether it was morning or evening. The light did not help.
I was walking in Oxford; the grey 16th Century walls
partially covered by green moss, guided my way.
The morning was brilliant, fine shafts of sunlight
pierced the narrow road between a cotton drapery of clouds
that moved lazily in no direction I could ascertain.
Feeling drugged, I walked past what had been a clinic
in the 17th Century, where Thomas Willis worked.
Or was it evening, much too late to have dinner
and my long, half-awakened day spent mostly in the red chair
almost over? Trying to sit outside, at least for part
of the time, as weak as I was, seemed necessary.
And I wanted to talk, seriously, to someone, to anyone.

Five

Difficult

Not for this last, not for adventure, nor mere exploration,
but to commit myself to the forms of love, save a life,
bring out of the mist a clarity that no pleasure
could obscure, no green forest could distract.
In fact, the forest was the essence, a sapling
that our lives yearned for, might only discover
in the dream out of meditation, the moment after
when, whatever world was present, it was not our world.
It was like trying to explain color to the blind,
or even to the color blind. Who knows what red means?
It had been forty years since I had seen this place,
long enough for memory to crystalize into dull form,
and for the inattentive to be swept away in the tide,
but not so long still for the truth of it to linger.

Six

Faith in healing, the ability of the body
to accomplish anything is a kind of reduction
that may lead to a new world. I mean, how
does our knowledge serve us when we know
that however much we've learned
we've remained where we began?
Is the only way through the darkest place,
and without guarantees? I had wanted guides.
Knowing you must heal yourself does not mean
you don't need help. All help should be gladly taken.
Outside my window, the wind strikes chimes
hanging from the great box elder. You do not see the wind,
but the question, after so much disappointment,
is do you see the chimes?

Seven

Look around less. Imagine more.
The man was sitting, slightly rocking,
on one of those old wooden porch chairs on hinges.
He motioned to me, pointing to the side of the porch.
It was a warm, typical Southern evening, with fireflies,
perfect, and the man noted my approval.
But if this was to be my Spirit-Guide,
he had to be completely silent,
had to originate from that shadow place,
a pure, blinding clarity in the dark,
where time and light merge, just
as I had always known.

Eight

I think I must have been a bird. Then maybe
a coatimundi. Then it gets blurry. They say I lost the tail last,
and then slowly became the beginnings of myself.
Somehow, being human didn't feel like a destination,
just a resting place on our way to the unknown region.
I can see brightly colored umbrellas off in the distance,
and the only choice is to stand with all humility
near this precipice and wonder what's next.

Nine

When I woke up this time, I was astonished to see
St. Thomas Aquinas standing over me.
I couldn't mistake him for anyone else, the robes, hat...
the rest just like the old paintings. He seemed a little ill at ease.
Well, I guess I was wrong, he said. I had to agree.
All that carefully reasoned theology jettisoned
like compost, as though the stench of centuries
could be made whole again, sparkling on a hill.

Ten

After Reading Faulkner's THE BEAR

Jerry taught me how to use a shotgun,
and together we went skeet shooting.
Never hunted, however, though once I remember
eating quail which he had shot that day.
We had to be careful because of the pellets
still embedded in the flesh.
Long ago my father was taken deer hunting
by the Hearst boys, and they tromped
through the open woods seeing nothing,
until, tired, my father wanted to rest under a large fir
while the others continued toward a place they knew.
He closed his eyes and probably dozed a little
until he heard a quiet rustle in the brush,
and, opening his eyes, saw a great, eight-pointed buck
standing ten feet from him, not moving.
He stared into the buck's eyes
which stared back into his own, quiet, fearless,
at home in his world. And then, without hurry,
he bounded away, and my father didn't stir.
Instead he said nothing to his friends and they went home.
It feels as though ninety years had passed in an instant,
and I had held the polished stock and cold metal.
And, come to think of it, perhaps I did.

Eleven

Dreaming is useful, handy when needed,
and I come out of this set
remembering little, but certain
of the clues given me
in that pine-scented forest I walked in.
So the only question I have left
is am I leaving the world
or drawing closer to it?

Twelve

Questions, always questions. I have them all the time
until it is actually time to ask; and then
they have blown away in soft wisps,
like early morning summer fog in Berkeley.
I stare at the white horizon, knowing
what seems impossible can be easily overcome,
but the static in my eyes prevents
my knowing, which is my form for seeing.
Today, though, I will be making up catfood,
and ghee for my wife, as well as holding on tightly
to the wiry fur and bright body of the lion.
How do I know this? Is this just nonsense? What does it serve?
Only: that for once in my life I am committing
to the real world, not the imagined illusion.

Thirteen

The Practice

Across the desert, the blue rolls out as far as you can see.
You don't follow it though that is one of many temptations.
You don't resist anything. Bitterbrush, mesquite, creosote bush
rustle in the wind but the blue remains.
It's as though you are in the middle of a long recuperation.
You lie down. You walk. You sit in the great red chair
most of the day trying to work it out. You can't.
The overwhelming drowsiness may be
due to drugs, but you can't trust that either.

In the little stone wall that appears on your left,
something out of place gleams white among the grey stones.
It is a simple matter to pull out a few above,
and then release it from the centuries it lay there.
A figure stands in front of a marble table,
or perhaps an altar. It is difficult to tell.
But in subsequent years it becomes my altar,
the worn and ancient, faceless figure my true self.

So that now the two of us manage the blue,
like an endless unrolling carpet in the Oz books. And yet,
I am going nowhere. Small wind devils whirl in the distance,
dried Rixford pods rattling in the wind are the only sound.
My life is being held by nothing that is common,
but everything is true. It would be so easy
to slip into the contemporary, to adapt the rhythms of the young.

Though every time I try to write nonsense,
I am prevented by the great wealth of the world.

The prophesies are dreadful, but tiny wren tits jump
from branch to branch on the trumpet vine.
Wind chimes begin a music harmonic, and dissonance,
though it has its place, is not the rule here.
The desert is blooming. Bright yellow blossoms
combine with the blue. Heart, Heart, I am crying out,
ready to settle in a land I cannot understand
but am willing to enter, my hands palms up,
my healing a distance apart, and certain.

Fourteen

How can a puma be a rock? Or history be tomorrow?
I have lived long enough to know these things
and have taken care to not mistake one for another.
Who then will guide me in the dark places?
A great block of stone tumbles clattering
through the bushes and small trees. Birds, alarmed,
fly over my head. They warn of nothing in particular,
but there is no sweetness in the fruit falling either.
It is all about balance, a handhold, or a ledge.
It is all about how my hand touches your forehead,
so tenderly, and permanently, just an infinitesimal spark
on a field of black. To believe in beauty is both fortunate
and necessary. We work with what we have,
no more, no less, and it is enough.

Fifteen

Poetry can't do it, unfortunately.
Nor painting, sculpture,
or novels. Maybe music.
For me, certainly.
Beyond that,
I don't know.

Sixteen

Talking about last things,
being reasonable about what is not,
drinking bone broth out on the deck
with a cool breeze under a hot August sun;
the fog is off to the west,
though I am facing east and the hills,
the warm dry grasses and browning leaves
click against each other and then
fall onto the flagstone.
How much time is there?
Scent of chicken baking
and basmati rice cooking.
The fig tree will once again
produce maybe one edible fruit –
it is just too cool here
for them to ripen fully,
though the squirrels will be happy.

My instructions are to sit.
If there is healing to be done,
it must be done through that door,
a threshold no one may see,
barriers we wouldn't notice anyway,
or through the difficult ones,
making conscious our struggle,
healing in a manner no one feels is possible,
yet everyone does it, not knowing what they do;
thinking how impossible it is to talk
one's way out of this trap, and so preparing,
we think we are preparing,
and so listening to the intelligent crows

conversing in the redwood two houses down.
Birds and soft winds, distant planes
making death seem impossible
or at the very least unreasonable.
How could a tree, or even a trumpet vine die?
Surely they are harbingers of a beauty
beyond any comprehension.

What if we had twenty or thirty senses,
not five? Would that help?
What if we had been pushing
our boat filled with what we thought
were our possessions, through a slough,
with no sure footing?
What if we fell exhausted on the dry deck
to wake the next morning in brilliant sunlight?
What if I could make this afternoon dozing
whole and clean, a life purified,
a miracle though not really so,
as it happens every day, conscious
as we are or not?

What if illness had no more use of me;
it had served its function and was no longer needed;
and how we can speak of last things
without real knowledge, but with a great desire;
knowing that history doesn't count,
and the way ahead is clear;
and I find myself by a great cascade,

the spray wetting my face,
the brilliant air and animals, all my friends
around me, guardian, gatekeeper,
my clarity unimpeded, leading
to an Amazon where no fear can disrupt,
no doubt can even register, much less disturb.

Seventeen

Primary Colors

Red, orange, yellow,
green, blue, purple, and white to
include them all. No, out in the world
they teach us otherwise.
But my heart tells me:
Go to the green.

Eighteen

Now I'm traveling on the caboose.
Though in my world
it takes me where I want to go,
its old, clacking body rattles and chuffs like a bear.
The landscape is not where it's been,
but where there are no tracks in the wilderness,
where the red-tailed hawk on the telephone pole
impassively watches me go by.
The old-fashioned car breathes with my breath.
When the long, mourning whistle blows,
I can lean back in the comfortable well-worn seat,
close my eyes and let the rocking
encourage me to sleep
yet be as attentive as I ever have been.

Nineteen

Happiness

I'm waiting in the car while Jane goes into the store
to pick up cat litter because these days I am not quite strong
enough to carry the bags, listening on the radio to a recording
of Mendelssohn's Scottish Symphony, looking out the window
and thinking of nothing until without warning
I'm seized by a joy so intense my eyes tear up,
and I'm shaking. It lasts only for a minute,
and then Jane comes back with the bags and we drive home.

Twenty

Another Guide

The bowing phantoms are like kelp swaying gently under water.
Eyeless, they motion to me, pain being a relative matter,
and all the experts with their medicinal smell
can do little except gaze mournfully while friends hover
and know better. It is so tempting to not tell anyone
anything, but then, quietness is the only ally I can trust,
sheep grazing on the hills under The Old Man,
a pika's sharp bark a clue, water and air: all combustible.

Twenty-one

You have to ask; purity, if that is what you want,
depends on it absolutely. Therefore
I am seated in this tiny study that once
was a one-car garage open in the back
but now is closed with three windows,
a decent plywood floor, a handmade desk
and a couple of chairs. Here will I make
my paradise, summon the spirits I must have.

Twenty-two

If there is no dissonance, only a greater defintion
of harmony; then the form must be accurate,
then the birds must come to the flower at exactly
the right time, to sip the juice which is energy;
which they do! Therefore, how can there be an ending,
how can there be oblivion; what rights do we claim?
The new wooden fence holds nothing back;
it simply clarifies what is there.

Twenty-three

The Explorer

They didn't choose me for my skill at dancing,
or for my unusual athletic ability.
Even if what I do has no intrinsic value,
well, what does? Why am I sitting here,
my bum sore, searching for something,
I don't even know what, pretending
to be Scott of the Antarctic, understanding vaguely
that beauty is all that matters?

Twenty-four

There is a sliding panel at the corner of my left eye,
so that when I look to the left it slides swiftly,
opening a new landscape, not the expected one
of house and deck, but rather something fantastic,
an arctic vision, ice and water, a crystal blue,
deep and unknowable, as though one could be swept
to the left and down, down, into the real self.
Impossible, I keep saying, until I realize nothing is.

Twenty-five

The Magnificent Tree

I am in mourning for my fallen tree, the hundred-plus-year-old
box elder that graced our back yard. With four trunks, on its own,
it made our yard into a forest. Now the critters that made it their home
on different levels, have packed their bags to find a new one.
Soon we will plant new trees, or flowers, or maybe a vegetable garden.
It will be fine, though for now I see the great tree's shadow,
tall and proud and alive as ever, the squirrels and woodpeckers
busy living their amazing lives, all of us together, partners in the world.

Twenty-six

Guests come. I can't tell if they are saving my life
or escorting me out of it. Their intentions
are the best and I feel constant love
flowing towards and into me.
They must be saving me. No other explanation
is possible, though the draining is palpable.
These days I have El Greco eyes, focusing hard
in the middle, furring out beyond those last trees.

Look look! The acorn woodpecker cackles, here,
in the middle of a Berkeley neighborhood.
Wildness seems far away, though remove these houses
and it's back here just as before, and my neighbor
laughing as always, each house on the block
filled with the robust dying and joyful living
the man in thick rubber boots
early fall rain, the plum trees closing down.

Bill Mayer was born and raised in Los Angeles. He received his BA and MA from San Francisco State University. Through much of his life, he was a dealer in fine wines, especially German and Austrian. He was an avid photographer, exhibiting his pictures of bristlecone pines in the White Mountains of eastern California at Mythos Gallery in 2011. His poetry has appeared in numerous literary journals and magazines. From 1992 to 2019, he published six books of poetry, among them *The Deleted Family* and *Articulate Matter*. He was married to the art historian, Jane McKinne-Mayer. He died after a long illness on October 25, 2019. *A Distance Apart*, his final poems, was written during the last months of his life.

www.ingramcontent.com/pod-product-compliance
Lightning Source LLC
Chambersburg PA
CBHW022000290426
44108CB00012B/1156